CLOSET SONNETS:
THE LIFE OF G.S. CROWN
(1950-2021)

Poems by Yakov Azriel

Closet Sonnets:
The Life of G. S. Crown
(1950-2021)

Sheep Meadow Press
Rhinebeck, New York

Designed and typeset by The Sheep Meadow Press
Distributed by The University Press of New England

Cover image: The Arch of Titus, Rome
Author Photograph: Meir Zarovsky

Library of Congress Cataloging-in-Publication Data

Names: Azriel, Yakov, 1950- author.
Title: Closet sonnets : the life of G.S. Crown, 1950-2021 / by Yakov Azriel.
Description: Rhinebeck, NY : The Sheep Meadow Press, 2017.
Identifiers: LCCN 2017015226 | ISBN 9781937679736 (pbk.)
Classification: LCC PS3601.Z75 C56 2017 | DDC 811/.6--dc23
LC record available at https://lccn.loc.gov/2017015226

All inquiries and permission requests should be addressed to the publisher:

The Sheep Meadow Press
PO Box 84
Rhinebeck, NY 12514

Dedicated to the memory of our father,
G.S. Crown (1950-2021)

Come! vouchsafe to me what has yet been vouchsafed to none—
Tell me the whole story,
Tell me what you would not tell your brother, wife …

                    —Walt Whitman

In fact, no matter where you go in the world, there is only one important story: of youth, and loss, and yearning for redemption. So we tell the same story, over and over again.

              —Rohinton Mistry, *Family Matters*

Acknowledgments

Various of these poems have appeared in the following magazines:

Cortland Review, Third Wednesday, Assaracus, Glitterwolf, Snakeskin, Impossible Archtype, and *Eleven Eleven*

CONTENTS

Preface   XV

Closet #1: 1960-1969

Adolescence   3
The High School Astronomer   3
High School Sophomore   4
The Honor Student   4
The High School Oceanographer   5
Eleventh Grade   5
One Moonlit Summer Night   6
Dreams Came To Me   6
High School Junior   7
On The Way To School   7
High School Senior   8
Twelfth Grade   8
Dating   9
High School Graduation   9
Perjury   10
Him   10
Shouldn't   11
As Soon As   11
The Nocturnal Bat   12
The Flutist   12
The First Time   13
When You Were Young   13

Closet #2: 1970-1979

Denial   17
Censored   17
Beware   18
Nuptials   18

"The Bedroom Scene"   19
The Leading Role   19
The Task   20
Winter Solstice   20
The King Of Comedy   21
The Negligee   21
La Place De La Concorde   22
Auto-Da-Fe   22
Sleuth   23
Onstage   23
His Hand   24
Mustn't   24

Closet #3: 1980-1989

Apollo's Dolphin   27
The Coral Reef   27
My Parents' Gift   28
Atlantis   28
Beneath   29
Mermen   29
Greek Symposium   30
The Runner   30
The Trojan War   31
Cassandra   31
The Cyclops   32
The Hellenist's Beach   32
In The Depths   33
Reality   33
Free Will   34
Don't Tell Me   34
A Siren Song   35
Apollo   35
Greek Tragedy   36
Satyr   36
Hellas   37
03:17 AM   37

Keeping A Secret 38
Moon Goddess 38
If You Were In My Shoes 39
Alphabet Soup 39
Listen 40
In The Park As Day Retreats 40
Miracle In Broad Daylight 41
The Mannequin 41
Somewhere 42
After 42
Closet Arithmetic 43
Bravery 43
Things Get Lost 44
Misplaced 44

Closet #4: 1990-1999

Breakfast Table 47
Dichotomy 47
The Martian 48
Welcome To Mars 48
Exploring Mars 49
Speaking Martian 49
Translating Martian 50
Introduction To Mars 50
Numbers 51
Free Association 51
The Gay Bar 52
Enlocked 52
How 53
Remembrance Of Things Past 53
Circling Mars 54
Solar System 54
Martian Music 55
Do Martians Dream? 55
Lucky Stars 56
Incantation 56

The Closet Library 57
The Looking-Glass 57
Modesty 58
The Specimen 58
Shut The Closet Door 59
Acceptance 59
Abomination 60
Prohibited 60
Percussion 61
The Penitentiary 61
Disapproval 62
Independence Day 62
The Purple Mockingbird 63
Perception 63

Closet #5: 2000-2009

Age 50 67
Old Enough 67
Wild Orchids 68
Taboo 68
Sharing 69
Luck 69
Bright Star 70
The Surf 70
Epistle 71
Communication 71
Consideration 72
Coronation 72
Supposed To 73
Where 73
The Follower 74
Lava 74
Tierra Del Fuego 75
Snowman 75
Spring 76
Beneath The Balcony 76

Wonderman   77
Not Here, Not Now   77
Better Left Unsaid   78
Beyond This Park   78
Riding The Dragon   79
Story Hour   79
The People Of The Day   80
The Neglected Orchard   80
The Science Of Desire   81
Splinter   81
Is That Too Much   82
For You, And About You   82

Closet #6: 2010-2021

Silence   85
The English Teacher   85
Family Man   86
The Professor   86
The Graduate Student   87
Mirror In The Closet   87
The Secret Garden   88
Compatriots   88
Grandpa   89
Who's There?   89
My Bedroom Walls   90
The Time-Bomb   90
Centaurs   91
Openness   91
The Accountant   92
Spelling Bee   92
Redemption   93
Alternative   93
In Order To Survive   94
Release   94
A Strange Device   95
Stuck   95

The Berlin Wall 96
Silence No More 96
The Outing 97
Investigation 97
What Will Remain? 98
We Are 98

PREFACE

Our father, G.S. Crown, died on his birthday, March 5, 2021, at the age of 71. Shortly after his death, we began sorting through his papers and came across a collection of hundreds of poems—all sonnets—which he never showed to any of us, and which we did not know existed. In these sonnets, our father was able to write about the closet in which he lived, a closet which we were all unaware of, and of the men he knew (or never knew). Our mother too was unaware of our father's secret gay life—a life he may have lived only in the closet of his life. Or maybe not.

After reading and re-reading Father's poems, we debated among ourselves if we should have them published or not. Another consideration was their number, since Father had written close to a thousand closet sonnets, and we realized that we could publish only a selected number of them.

Why did Father write sonnets? We don't know, of course, and he is not here to tell us the reason. Perhaps the tight, locked form of the sonnet mirrors the tight, locked closet in which he lived.

This book is therefore a selection of our father's sonnets—about closets, shadows, Apollo's dolphin, mermen and Mars, arranged according to the decades of his life.

May they serve as his memorial.

—The family
March, 2024

CLOSET #1: 1960-1969

ADOLESCENCE

I don't remember when I first began
to knock upon a closet door or when
not pretty girls but college boys and men
began to populate my dreams. One man
invited me to tea, a second ran
to buy me wine, a third prepared me ten
delicious kinds of homemade pie and then
he brought me gingerbread and marzipan.

I don't remember very much, but still
one memory persists: I asked the stars
why I was so unlike the boys I went
to high school with. I asked and asked until
one planet answered me, the planet Mars,
in whose red desert I have pitched my tent.

THE HIGH SCHOOL ASTRONOMER

I used to ask the stars to tell me why
I was so different from the boys I went
to high school with. I wondered, to what extent
were faulty chromosomes the reason I
would open up locked closet doors and pry
inside? Was this a kind of punishment
for sins I did? And was this permanent
or passing, like a comet in the sky?

I told the stars I wanted very much
to be like all my friends, to someday find
a woman I would love, to someday be
a father, too. I thought the stars could touch
the human soul, transform the human mind;
I didn't know they dream all night like me.

HIGH SCHOOL SOPHOMORE

The way my English teacher speaks to me—
the way he says my name—the way he looks
at me—the way he recommends thick books
he thinks I would enjoy—the way that he
suggests I read Walt Whitman's poetry—
the way he casts a net—the way he hooks
a fishing rod—the way he overcooks
the fish he's caught in bonfires by the sea—

as if he found my beach—as if he knew
my bay—as if he saw how much I wish
I didn't have a closet—from the way
he looks at me, he has a closet too,
a closet with an ocean full of fish—
as if he sensed my fear of being gay—

THE HONOR STUDENT

I was a quiet boy who studied for
examinations, did his homework, learned
to conjugate French verbs by heart, and earned
a string of "A"s for papers on Lahore
in West Punjab, what makes a muscle sore,
the structure of the atom, when Troy was burned
by Greeks, and how Napoleon returned
to France. But what about my closet's shore?

Although at school no science teacher taught
us that behind a closet door a sea
existed, full of eddies, waiting to
engulf a careless swimmer, I was caught
inside a whirling maelstrom, pulling me
beneath strong waves, not knowing what to do.

4

THE HIGH SCHOOL OCEANOGRAPHER

Not knowing what to do about the sea
behind my closet door, I made believe
it wasn't there; perhaps I was naïve
to think that certain things just have to be
and certain things can never be. For we
were taught in school no closet could conceive
an ocean, and salt water had to cleave
to laws of inorganic chemistry.

We also learned a "normal" boy is not
attracted to another boy, and love
belongs to couples married properly.
But what about my sea? No matter what
our textbooks said, I heard the roaring of
its waves, I heard a merman calling me.

ELEVENTH GRADE

I heard a merman asking me to swim
with him; he looked exactly like the man
who had approached me on the beach. "I'm Stan,"
he said, "I noticed you're alone." "I'm Jim,
my girlfriend's coming soon," I answered him.
He sighed and left. But afterwards I ran
along the shore, remembering his tan,
his gait, his torso, muscular and slim.

For weeks and months I heard the crashing of
the surf inside my closet, night by night,
and saw a merman waiting on the sand.
A solitary seagull flew above
him as my closet's lighthouse poured its light
upon the merman stretching forth his hand.

ONE MOONLIT SUMMER NIGHT

One moonlit summer night you first began
to sense how oceans ebbed and flowed inside
your closet, oceans which you had to hide
from everyone you knew. There was a man
who charted all those seas, a man you ran
away from, fearing his embrace. He eyed
you in the closet, but he knew to bide
his time, as if he had a master-plan.

The navigator whom you dreamt of knew
that you were one of us; he knew the tide,
the surf, the truth, the lapping waves that tease
us in our dreams would pull you in, that you
belonged to him, that he would be your guide
to beaches lining all your closet's seas.

DREAMS CAME TO ME

Dreams came to me like owls, to build a nest
behind my closet door; dreams came to me
like wrens at twilight searching for a tree
where they could spend the night, where they could rest
secure and safe from cats. When I repressed
my dreams, these dreams returned as bees, each bee
intent on stinging something else: my knee,
my elbow or my neck, my back, my chest.

Dreams came to me like stubborn ghosts that clasp
a mirror in their hands and cry, "Behold
thyself, behold thy visage in the light
of truth"—my dreams of mermen who would grasp
me in their arms and pull me towards the cold
yet strangely welcome ocean of the night.

HIGH SCHOOL JUNIOR

The guys I go to high school with enjoy
four-lettered words. The seniors always curse
the juniors and the juniors reimburse
them with long lists of insults that annoy
our teachers but eventually destroy
a schoolboy's self-esteem. There's nothing worse
in all these curses, nothing more adverse
than "hey, homo!"—a boy who's not a boy.

Should any of my classmates find the sea
I hide from them, or come across the sand
that lines my closet's shore, or ever hear
a merman in my closet calling me
to pull him up by stretching out my hand,
my only friend will be an empty pier.

ON THE WAY TO SCHOOL

Aboard a crowded bus, the man who sat
beside me pressed his thigh against my thigh,
he rubbed his leg against my leg. And I
did not resist—how can an alley cat
resist a piece of fish, how can a rat
resist a slice of cheese, how can a fly
resist a drop of milk, how can a lie
resist the flesh of truth it's staring at?

The man began to breathe unevenly—
he placed his hand atop my thigh as well—
I rang the bell and quickly left the bus;
I ran to school, pretending not to see
his face, pretending not to hear the bell
which signaled "class dismissed" for both of us.

HIGH SCHOOL SENIOR

A locker room is not the place for guys
like us, for guys who are afraid we'll stare
at friends when they undress, for guys who fear
a passerby might notice what our eyes
are focused on, for guys who fantasize
that friend we're staring at will nod and share
his shower stall, for guys who dare not dare;
a locker room is not a place for lies.

And yet a locker room is just the place
for us, a soccer field in which we play
without our clothes, a tennis court where we
can give the shadows from our dreams a face,
a body and a ball. And yesterday
I saw a high school junior stare at me.

TWELFTH GRADE

At twilight, shadows admonish me, "You're not
a boy, you are a man, you have the right
to close your books, to walk outside and light
a cigarette, to find the truth of what
you need according to your dreams. You've got
to wrestle with an angel and to fight
him till the morning, even though the night
you struggle in is humid, long and hot."

The shadows pull me to a window where
I see the evening star. "Just listen to
the stars, it's time to throw away your mask,
to throw away your glasses, too. Don't fear
night's questions or its question marks, are you
a schoolboy or a man?" the shadows ask.

DATING

The pretty girls I date must wonder why
I never ask to kiss them when I take
them home, or hold their hand, or try to make
a pass at them. Perhaps they think I'm shy
or overly polite, not knowing I
conceal a closet with a sleeping snake
inside, a cobra which I mustn't wake,
for once aroused, he'll slither up my thigh.

If I go out with pretty girls, perhaps
I'll somehow change and fall in love with one
of them. Not very likely, though, for when
I dream, all bolted closet doors collapse
and there I stand, beneath a summer sun
with cobras on a beach, and naked men.

HIGH SCHOOL GRADUATION

The shadows pull me to a closet where
I'm told I should unlock its door and see
vast oceans stretching towards infinity.
Along the beachfront is a wooden pier
on which I walk, a fishing dock I share
with dozens of twelfth-graders who, like me,
are still uncertain if they ought to be
a merman or a fisherman of fear.

So what am I supposed to do? To dive
and drown, or dive and swim? To dive until
I touch the ocean floor? I am afraid
to die, I am afraid I might survive,
I am afraid the ocean's salt will fill
my lungs the moment that I leave twelfth grade.

PERJURY

Don't tell your father or your mother or
your brothers what you feel; you must deny
you swim with shadows in the night; you lie
not only to poor Banquo's ghost, the Moor
of Venice and the prince of Elsinore,
but also to yourself; you even cry
there is no witness who can testify
a sea exists behind your closet door.

You swear before the wind, the sand, the shore,
the moon, the stars, the ocean's ebb and flow
no shadows ever stroke your hair, your eyes,
your body or your soul. You swear before
your closet's waves in vain; the wind will blow
away the sand that covers all your lies.

HIM

Don't think of him. Don't close your eyes and see
him in your mind. Don't hope he'll come. Don't say
his name or even jot it down. Don't stay
awake at night, imagining that he
will hear your music in the dark. Don't be
obsessed by him, don't fantasize one day
he'll play a flute duet with you. Don't pray
for something he would say is blasphemy.

You know you mustn't ever tell him what
you feel. You know you mustn't ever tell
him what you dream about. Don't try to rhyme
his name with yours, don't jump into a pot
of boiling oil, don't leap into a well
whose walls are much too slippery to climb.

SHOULDN'T

I know I shouldn't think of him this way,
I know I shouldn't stay awake at night
invoking him, imagining he might
be swimming in my closet's sea. Today
I'll speak to him, I tell myself, he may
agree to come ashore, he may delight
in knowing what I feel, he may not fight
the tides; stay with me, I'll whisper, stay, stay.

I know I shouldn't think of him like this,
but still I do. Immersed in what I see,
I watch the surf—the more I stare, the more
I spot him waving, coming. Waters kiss
the sand, embrace the waiting rocks; how free
the ocean is, how happy is the shore.

AS SOON AS

The truth? As soon as he appears, I stare
at him. I stare, and hope he doesn't see
my stare. The truth? Although there's nowhere we
could share a life with one another here
on Earth or on a distant planet where
I needn't fear the truth, as soon as he
appears my mask of anonymity
and all my hiding-places disappear.

The truth? It's staring in my face as soon
as he appears.   A comet in the sky
inscribes my name in red as all my fears
come true: the sun collapses and the moon
explodes, exposing me; there's nowhere I
can hide—nowhere!—as soon as he appears.

THE NOCTURNAL BAT

he looked at me   i looked at him   he came
a little haltingly to sit astride
an empty bench   he sighed   i also sighed
(*what flew above our heads? pale hunters aim
 their guns in readiness to shoot their game*)
"it's lovely here," he said   "oh, yes," i lied
"perhaps you have a place where we—," he tried
to talk, but couldn't, overcome by shame

(*a place? i am a bat, i'm neither fish
nor fowl; because i fly, all mammals shun
my presence—yet, no bird agrees to stay
with me as well   more hunters come   i wish
i didn't hear the shooting of a gun*)
i answered, "no"   he sighed and walked away

THE FLUTIST

"*you play the flute?*"   i nodded yes   he smiled
"*we'll play together then?*"   i nodded yes
his skillful fingers started to caress
my chest, my stomach and below   a wild,
ferocious lion roared   a little child
began to cry   i didn't care   "*undress*,"
he said, "*so that our music can express
a paradise that's pure and undefiled*"

we found a shaded garden suitable
for our duet of piccolo and flute
i placed my lips and tongue upon his skin
how lithe his body was   as beautiful
and naked as a snake   forbidden fruit
and i, a son of adam, tasted sin

THE FIRST TIME

How simple. As simple as A B C
He stared. I stared. He came closer. D E
We talked a bit, of this and that. F G
Finally he asked, "Will you come with me?"
"Yes." H I J K L M N O P
He led me to his star. Q R S T
He led me to his galaxy. U V
His universe. W X Y Z

But then the letters tumbled down. H K
F W M S—they don't obey
the rules the way they did before. Today
the alphabet has changed, its letters sway
and shuffle, back and forth R X O J
How complicated it is C B A

WHEN YOU WERE YOUNG

You heard the shadows in your closet speak
to you when you were young, you heard them say
your name. They told you not to turn away
and not to be afraid, but take a peek
behind the closet door and even sneak
inside, to dance. You heard them day by day,
week by week, month by month; to your dismay,
you also felt their fingers touch your cheek.

At first you tried ignoring them, you tried
to make believe you didn't hear, you cast
aside your ears throughout your early youth,
you cast aside the dusk, you cast aside
the closet key they brought. But now, at last,
you can accept the shadows spoke the truth.

CLOSET #2: 1970-1979

CENSORED

i dream of men who   *CUT*   i dream of men
as luminous as suns, but like the sun,
i mustn't stare at them   instead, i run
away from dawn   from noon   from day   for when
there's light, I yearn to   *CUT* and *CUT* again
i don't know what is 'fun'   is daylight 'fun'?
does light imply that one may   *CUT* , that one
is free of scissors and a censor's pen?

perhaps it's best to cut my eyeballs out
to stab them hard   to throw them to the ground
to cut out private body parts and shut
them in a closet where i'll never shout
their names   for when your life revolves around
a pair of scissors, you are   *CUT* *CUT* *CUT*

DENIAL

You can deny the facts. You can deny
the simplest truths. You can deny you're gay.
Just as you can deny the Milky Way
is made of stars, or supernovas die
once they've exploded, or the number pi
is infinite; you can deny the day
is followed by the night. But though you say
a lie is true, a lie remains a lie.

So go ahead, get married, claim you love
your wife; so go ahead and give her bread
you cannot bake. You can deny you run
around in circles at the bottom of
a pit you've dug yourself—yes, go ahead
deny the sky, deny the moon and sun.

BEWARE

Beware the man you are—a man who hides
tall shadows in his closet, gray by gray,
black by black, white by white; a man who's gay
but won't admit he's gay, a man who bides
his time in vain. You shouldn't fear the Ides
of March, you should beware the Ides of May,
a sunny afternoon, your wedding day,
carnations and white dresses worn by brides.

Beware the whispers people share behind
your back, beware the horse, beware the cart
you put before the horse, beware the car
that races down the street, beware the mind
which can deduct the truth, beware the heart,
beware the stars that made you as you are.

NUPTIALS

Why does a bride wear white? She ought to wear
a gown of varied grays, for married life
is neither white nor black. The future wife
may someday learn her husband didn't share
with her how lions stalk his dreams, or dare
reveal the truth about his closet, rife
with shadowed panthers, and the bowie knife
beneath a boulder in a leopard's lair.

Wear gray, I would advise the bride, wear gray
for married life is neither black nor white.
Like truth. Like love. Do all the many shades
of gray imply her husband will betray
her like a tiger prowling in the night?
The night grows wilder as gray twilight fades.

"THE BEDROOM SCENE"

It's hard to be an actor and pretend
that you're a character you're not. The scene
I find the hardest is the one between
my wife and me, "THE BEDROOM SCENE." We end
up in our bed without our clothes, I bend
my body over hers, I even lean
and speak of passion, but it doesn't mean
a thing—what only shadows comprehend.

How hard it is, the act of making love,
of showing her what other husbands show
their wives. In fact, it's all a show, for when
I stroke her flesh, I'm really thinking of
the men I cannot touch; she doesn't know
I'm thinking of the flesh of naked men.

THE LEADING ROLE

The play continues on and on, but it
is difficult for me to play the role
of loving husband every night. I stroll
upon the stage, reciting lines that fit
the part, but merely mouth my words. I spit
upon myself because I know my soul
has been dichotomized, no longer whole;
am I an actor, or a hypocrite?

How long until the curtain falls? How long
will I pretend to be what I am not?
How long must I deceive and trick my wife?
My lies are daggers actors use. It's wrong,
I know, to stab her in the dark, but what
am I to do? My role demands a knife.

19

THE TASK

I somehow manage to perform the task
a husband must perform; I close my eyes
and make believe it is a man who lies
beneath me, not my wife. She mustn't ask
for more than that because I need a mask
when I lie naked and a good disguise
when I undress, to help me minimize
the fact my bottle is an empty flask.

I close my eyes, pretending it's a man
my hands are stroking now, a man that I've
embraced, for only men arouse me in
the way I need to be aroused. How can
I keep deceiving her? How can I dive
into a flask devoid of wine or gin?

WINTER SOLSTICE

If I divulge the truth to her—I think
my truth would freeze her heart if I would show
her all my closet's snowmen and the snow
I build them from, the snow I thaw and drink
when she's away—if I turn ice to ink
and with that ink, transcribe the truth, then go
and publicize it all, she'd finally know
her husband's icicle is colored pink.

How can I do this to my wife? How can
I throw the winter at her when she thinks
that spring exists? She doesn't find the sled
I hide, she doesn't see what kind of man
I am, or how a thirsty snowman drinks
my melted ice while lying on our bed.

THE KING OF COMEDY

By now don't people realize nothing that
they see onscreen is true, that everything
is just a vaudeville show? My wedding ring
is plastic, and the laughing clown, so fat
and jolly, cries behind the camera. At
the stroke of midnight, people see the king
of comedy—that's me, of course; I bring
my crown as well: a Charlin Chaplin hat.

My regal robe is a soiled blanket and
my throne—a sagging bed, while every night
a pie is thrown directly in my face.
Quite funny, no? But on the other hand,
a jester or a fool may bring to light
the reason why a shadow fell from grace.

THE NEGLIGEE

Last night I died again. I must have died
a hundred times, since every time I lie
with her, pretending to make love, I die.
She's not aware of it because I slide
my corpse beneath the mattress or I hide
it in the closet where the shadows try
to resurrect my body as they cry,
believing I've committed suicide.

She's putting on the negligee she wore
last night. That only means one thing. I see
the scaffold and the hangman's noose. The men
who'll blindfold my eyes. The gallows' trapdoor.
Prepare the shroud. Prepare the eulogy.
Prepare the grave. Tonight I'll die again.

LA PLACE DE LA CONCORDE

She wore the negligee she wears when she
decides it's time for making love. So when
she put it on last night, I counted ten
and held my breath—to no avail, for we
made love. When we make love, she touches me—
my body lies inert—but then—and then—
(and all the while, my mind is full of men,
—undressed of course—emerging from the sea).

She smiled this morning when she woke; for her
it was a pleasant night. She hasn't seen
the headlines in the papers: *HUSBAND DEAD—*
a witness says the executioner
was swift—the blade was sharp—the guillotine
—ONE, TWO, THREE—severed body from the head.

AUTO-DA-FE

Do you want the truth? I lied last night. I lied
because I told her I desire to lie
with her. Each time I tell this lie, I sigh
a silent sigh; last night again I sighed,
last night again I told this lie. I cried
as well, in silence, since I always cry
when we make love. When we make love I die.
Auto-da-fe. Last night again I died.

Last night again I died by fire. I'm brought
before the Inquisition where I'm stripped
of all my clothes; as we make love, they take
me to be burned. But first, the whips. I ought
to be quite used to this, this being whipped
with thorns before they burn me at the stake.

SLEUTH

She doesn't see the footprints, doesn't see
the different hints and clues that march across
our bedroom floor, undress themselves and toss
their underwear upon our sheets. And she
ignores the feathers on our bed—so we
continue as before. I'm at a loss
how anyone can miss the albatross
which perches on my shoulder, pecking me.

A person only sees what she or he
expects to see; I know that she expects
to see a happy married life, the life
she's always dreamt about. But I can't be
the husband she desires, who disinfects
the nests of albatrosses for his wife.

ONSTAGE

There's very little I can do except
pretend I'm straight, pretend good-looking guys
don't interest me at all, pretend my eyes
don't gaze at them. Although I'm quite adept
at lying, shadows aren't—yet they've kept
my secret nicely, not revealing lies
I'm telling even as the curtains rise
when I perform on stages shadows swept.

I sometimes feel that I deserve a prize
for 'Actor of the Year,' that I deserve
at least one Oscar for the roles I play:
"devoted father," "faithful husband," "wise,
sagacious scholar." Shadows sway and swerve
behind the curtains, shadows swerve and sway.

HIS HAND

he placed his hand upon my hand   he placed
his hand upon my neck   he placed his hand
beneath my shirt, to make me understand
he wanted me   i nodded yes, and faced
his smile   he placed his hand upon my waist
he placed his hand, so muscular and tanned,
quite firmly on my bolt of lightning   and
it rained   then in the downpour, we embraced

but afterwards, i shoved his hand away
for if his hand had stayed, it would have cost
my family too much   too much   i shoved
his hand aside, i couldn't let them pay
the price for who i am   and so i lost
the One i loved, the One i almost loved

MUSTN'T

i mustn't think about his arms   his eyes
his chest   i mustn't wake up in the night
imagining he'll see my window's light
and come to me   i mustn't fantasize
the stars will nod approval if he lies
beside me in my bed   i mustn't write
this poem   i mustn't speak the truth, despite
the truth   i mustn't dream he strokes my thighs

i mustn't ever let him know the way
i feel   i mustn't smile   i mustn't pray
that God will have compassion and forgive
forbidden fantasies   i mustn't stay
too close to where he stands   i mustn't say
his name or gaze at him   i mustn't live

CLOSET #3: 1980-1989

APOLLO'S DOLPHIN

It's wrong of me to stare at you this way,
imagining how you must look when you're
undressed, imagining my fingers tore
your shirt and slowly stroked your chest. I lay
my hands upon your shoulders as you say
you want my hands to dive below, explore
your sea and throw our pants upon the shore.
I nod my head and eagerly obey.

Apollo's dolphin, who is looking at
the two of us, now nods his head. It's wrong
of me to stare at you this way; I fight
imagination, but the dolphin that
is blessing us seems powerful and strong,
assuring me it's perfectly all right.

THE CORAL REEF

Apollo's dolphin winks at me in dreams;
he promises there's nothing wrong with me
and swears it's quite respectable to be
attracted to athletic men. He seems
to have great wisdom, wisdom that redeems
me from the desert of my shame. *"You'll see
a coral reef,"* he says, *"where liberty
and freedom glow, where self-acceptance gleams."*

"Immerse," the dolphin urges me, *"and play
with me beneath my ocean, you will find
much ecstasy if you just grab my tail
and swim with me beyond this shallow bay."*
But is this true? I can't make up my mind
if he's a dolphin or a killer whale.

MY PARENTS' GIFT

My father and my mother gifted me
a coat of many colors—yellow, red,
green, purple, orange, blue. I saw each thread
was woven with much love, much sanctity,
in honor of their parents' memory.
They wanted me to treasure it. Instead,
I wore it when I took a loaf of bread
to feed Apollo's dolphin by the sea.

"Take off your coat," the grinning dolphin said,
*"who needs a coat of many colors when
my ocean is so warm; the other men
are naked in my sea."* I went ahead
and left it on the shore—but even then
I knew I'd never wear this coat again.

ATLANTIS

I open up my closet door. Within
the closet, winding pathways lead me to
a large lagoon. I swim beyond the blue
and shallow bay by grabbing tight the fin
a dolphin offers me; how masculine
he is, how strong. As we descend, a few
kind mermen take me by the hand, to view
their home, Atlantis, as they stroke my skin.

These mermen are all muscular, all sleek,
all interested in me; it's very queer
how interested they are. Am I asleep,
Atlantis just a dream? The light is weak
and growing weaker in Atlantis, where
my father's sun is swallowed by the deep.

BENEATH

Beneath my closet's floor there flows a sea,
an ocean stretching to Atlantis where
the mermen whom I dream of dwell. How near
Atlantis is, its ocean seems to be
right here, its waves are pounding steadily,
incessantly beneath my feet, right here
beneath my closet's floor. If I could tear
away the floor, the ocean would break free.

How far away Atlantis is, as far
away as memory. I met a man
and since that night, the waves I hear are his,
the brine I taste is his, the distant star
I see is his. Is there a chance he can
be mine? How far away Atlantis is.

MERMEN

I sometimes fantasize that he and I
could settle in Atlantis; living there
together as an ordinary pair
of mermen, we would never need to lie
to anyone again or to deny
emotions that we feel. Without the fear
of being caught or being branded queer,
we'd learn to live without the wind and sky.

I'd soon adjust to living there without
my mother's moon, without my father's sun,
without their stars I can't obey, as free
as whales that cruise the sea. But what about
my children? For Atlantis is a one
way trip. Apollo's dolphin laughs at me.

GREEK SYMPOSIUM

Most people find it hard to understand
the grammar of the language that I speak.
My native tongue is Greek, the ancient Greek
Achilles spoke, that Dionysus and
Poseidon sang, the language that a band
of earnest shadows in my bedroom seek
to resurrect; my language is the creak
of closet doors and footsteps on the sand.

In temples of Apollo, naked priests
conversed in it all night, the mermen of
Atlantis chanted it and there are men
alive today who drink its wine in feasts
that honor love, forbidden love, the love
of man for man, reviving Greek again.

THE RUNNER

Whoever you are, know I dream of you;
Whoever you are, know that late at night
I get up, tip-toe to the closet, light
a match—and there I see you running through
the darkness I created, running to
embrace me warmly, running to invite
me to come join your marathon and fight
the Trojans Lord Achilles never slew.

To fight the Trojans and to be a Greek,
to run like you, to overcome my fear
of who I am, to run until I reach
the bay where runners meet, where we can speak
to one another, man to man, and bare
the truth at last, together on that beach.

THE TROJAN WAR

The Trojans hate the Greeks; they are afraid
the Greeks may find a means to penetrate
the walls of Troy or sabotage the gate
protecting her from men whose ways degrade
time-honored Trojan laws, from Greeks who trade
with mermen on the beach. The Trojans hate
the Greeks and fear that Greece may enervate
their city with Greek shadows and Greek shade.

They hate the Greeks, whose customs circumvent
the straight and narrow Trojan paths. So Troy
has built enormous towers that reach the sky,
defending all her walls. So Troy has sent
her soldiers to the seashore, to destroy
the Grecian fleet. But can Greek shadows die?

CASSANDRA

Am I a Trojan or a Greek? Am I
a faithful citizen of Troy, whose wall
of massive stone was built to keep out all
disloyal soothsayers who prophesy
no city wall is thick enough or high
enough to thwart the Greeks, and Troy will fall?
Am I a Greek? Can I deny I call
on Daedalus to teach me how to fly?

Cassandra knows the truth, of course, but who
can hope to understand the words she sings,
and who can comprehend her prophecy?
She peers into my eyes—within their blue
she sees my soul, and rings within its rings—
she shakes her head—Cassandra, sing to me!

31

THE CYCLOPS

Two eyes are sometimes not as good as one;
for if a Cyclops comes, he'll understand
exactly who I am, not fooled by sand
which covers up my tracks or by the ton
of makeup on my face. How can I run
away? He'll catch me, grab me by the hand,
demolish all my closets and demand
I stand exposed beneath the midday sun.

A Cyclops is afraid of water, though;
he has a phobia of puddles, streams,
swamps, rivers, lakes, and most of all, the sea.
The sea! If only I could dive below
its surface, safe at last from Cyclops screams,
from Cyclops fingers coarsely fondling me.

THE HELLENIST'S BEACH

Some parents argue mermen don't exist
and claim Atlantis is a myth. They teach
their sons there is no isolated beach
where dolphins dance at dusk. Although a mist
has risen from the ocean, they insist
we cannot comprehend a dolphin's speech
nor can a modern sailing vessel reach
the vanished islands of the Hellenist.

These parents are mistaken, for I've met
a merman on this beach, a merman who
revealed Atlantis is as real as Rome,
as Paris or New York; my skin is wet
from swimming in his sea. According to
Apollo's dolphin, Atlantis is my home.

IN THE DEPTHS

I met a merman from Atlantis who
was kind enough to teach me how to swim
beneath the ocean waves; I clung to him
as we descended deeper, deeper to
the bottom of the sea where very few
landlubbers ever go. I held his slim,
aquatic body in my arms; how dim
the seafloor was, how bright the joy I knew.

But then my merman disappeared; he swam
from me one night in search of someone else:
a younger man, a better-looking man.
By now he's far away from where I am—
beyond the Bosporus and Dardanelles,
beyond Korea, China and Japan.

REALITY

It's getting difficult to separate
my fantasies from dry reality.
Nevertheless, I'm certain there's a sea
within my closet where kind mermen wait
at dusk to teach me how to navigate
strong underwater currents, how to be
as uninhibited as them, as free
as rolling waves that don't pretend they're straight.

Who cares if I develop gills? Instead
of air I'll breathe saltwater, while I learn
the customs of Atlantis and perceive
a realm of liberty my teachers said
is myth, but I'm convinced the sea I yearn
for is reality, not make believe.

FREE WILL

When looking back upon the choices we
have made, it's hard to know if they were wise
or not. I don't possess Apollo's eyes
which can foresee the future prison key
each choice creates. If he had given me
his vision, maybe I'd have thrown my lies
beyond the ocean's tides, and fraternize
with mermen in Apollo's dolphin's sea.

If I had chosen to go swimming in
the dolphin's sea, my daughter and my sons
would never have been born. I cannot make
that choice. I can't. It's better to have been
the shadows' prisoner, a man who runs
in circles at the bottom of a lake.

DON'T TELL ME

Don't tell me you've explored my closet, too.
Don't tell me you have opened up its door
and found Greek tunics ancient Spartans swore
they wouldn't wear again, as good as new
and wanting to be worn. Don't tell me you
unearthed a coin beneath the closet floor,
a coin which had survived the Trojan War
and doesn't bend, no matter what you do.

Don't tell me that this coin you found beneath
the closet has Atlantis stamped upon
it or that on the other side you see
Apollo's portrait with a laurel wreath.
Don't tell me that you've tried a tunic on,
don't tell me that you might end up like me.

A SIREN SONG

We're not allowed to dream about the sea.
Behind our closet door, we're not allowed
to dream about a merman who is proud
of having swum the Dardanelles, while we
have tied our hands with ropes and cannot free
ourselves. We're not allowed to touch a cloud,
or hope to swim the Bosporus, or crowd
around a shadow who says he found a key.

One shadow claims he's found a key that might
be able to unlock our closet door.
Is he a prophet or a siren or
a startled dreamer who woke up one night
and can't fall back to sleep? There's nothing more
seductive than a dream we must ignore.

APOLLO

Apollo—sir—you must remember I'm
a mortal, not a god like you. You must
remember to be patient, for I'm just
a human being. Your golden stallions climb
the sky, allowing you to master time,
forever young, eternally robust
and virile. Sir, how graciously you thrust
your gilded javelin, lustrous and sublime.

Although you're perfect, sir, without defect
or fault, I cannot be your paramour;
I have a wife, I have my children, too,
who all depend on me and don't suspect
you're standing nude behind my closet door.
Forgive me, sir, I cannot worship you.

GREEK TRAGEDY

A tragic hero has a tragic flaw
preventing him from finding happiness
or giving happiness. He cannot bless
the ones he loves, molested by the paw
of Destiny, a gorgon no one saw
until it was too late. He can't possess
a spear or sharpened sword, yet nonetheless
he'll battle Fate, despite the gorgon's claw.

My tragedy resides within my pants.
I know my wife had always hoped to live
a life enkindled by warm flames, a life
of ardent fire. The passion that she wants,
that she deserves, is something I can't give—
I love her as a sister, not a wife.

SATYR

I didn't plan to be the kind of man
I am. I didn't plan to live behind
a heavy closet door and live the kind
of life I'm living now. I didn't plan
I would discover that a closet can
contain extensive forests where I'd find
a naked, wiry satyr who reclined
beneath a terebinth, the satyr Pan.

I didn't plan to be enchanted by
his shepherd's flute, his pipe of reeds, his lyre;
to follow him at twilight to his cave;
to let his hands undress me and to lie
with him, intoxicated by desire—
O Pan! I didn't plan to be your slave.

HELLAS

The ancient Greeks would understand. A Greek
like Sophocles acknowledges that Fate
prepares a path which seemingly is straight
but twists a thousand times. They know how weak
we are, how easily we stray; they speak
of woodland roads from which we deviate.
Euripides would never castigate
my gazing at Apollo's bare physique.

Yet in the end, it's not Apollo, but
it's Pan who reappears, who takes me by
the hand to shadowed forests as his boy,
his playmate in the dark. And in his hut
he makes me swear: "May a Cyclops pluck my eye
if I forget thee, Pan, my chiefest joy."

03:17 AM

I wake up in the middle of my dreams—
wild dreams of naked men. I thought that I
could overcome all tempest winds the sky
would send me, overcome all sharp extremes
of noon and twilight, overcome all beams
of moonlight, overcome all ropes that tie
my hands and feet to flotsam drifting by
and overcome all overflowing streams.

God knows I want to be a "normal" man
who has a normal wife whom he can love
emotionally and physically. Instead
the Truth has other plans, like sending Pan
to me at night to play his flute above
my pillow, satyrs prancing on my bed.

KEEPING A SECRET

Who can I trust to tell my secret to?
I dare not tell my wife, my children or
my parents that behind my closet door
the satyr Pan likes playing peek-a-boo
with me. I dare not tell them what we do
together in the satyr's cave before
I fall asleep, or that he's getting more
and more demanding each time we rendezvous.

Who can I tell my secret to? If I
reveal it to a bee, the entire hive
will know. If I reveal it to the sun,
my family will burn. I can't rely
on mountains, they would bury us alive.
My secret isn't safe with anyone.

MOON GODDESS

Sweet Artemis, who changes every night,
who never stays the same, please change me, too;
I vow that if I change, I'll worship you.
Sweet Artemis, please change my sense of sight
so that my eyes might focus on the light
of women, not the light of men. Subdue
Apollo's dolphin, let your moon pursue
the sun and change its red to lunar white.

It's sometimes hard to worship Artemis;
it sometimes seems as if she doesn't hear
my prayers at all—as if she can't unlock
a closet door or see how dark it is
inside—as if the goddess doesn't care—
as if the moon were just a barren rock.

IF YOU WERE IN MY SHOES

If you were in my shoes, what would you do?
Would you betray your wife and search for men
who might agree to share your bed? And when
the morning came and they abandoned you,
would you return to her? A dragon flew
across the sky last week, he came again
last night. At first I was afraid, but then
I saw one talon trying on my shoe.

I told the dragon that I can't betray
my wife, nor can I even tell her that
it's men, it's only men I dream about.
The dragon listened but he didn't say
a word. Instead, he flapped his wings and spat
on me—the spit of fire, the fire of doubt.

ALPHABET SOUP

Confessions: (A) I live in a closet. (B)
I hide Fact A from everyone I know.
(C) Though closet soil is sandy, I grow
potatoes, carrots and onions there. (D)
I raise my crops beside my closet's sea.
(E) I watch the mermen who come and go
along this shore. (F) Robust mermen show
me learning how to swim might set me free.

(G) I make believe I'm not closet-gay.
(H) I make believe these mermen won't take
my crops. (I) I make believe I don't feel
a longing for my closet's ocean. (J)
I make believe this isn't true, I make
believe my closet's mermen aren't real.

LISTEN

Listen—the mist is calling you, the dew,
the fog, the vapors on a window pane.
The trees are calling you, the grass, the rain
that waters them and streamlets flowing through
your closet's forest, listen; buses, too,
and taxi-cabs across the street, a plane
which circles overhead, a distant train
you barely see or hear are calling you.

Listen well—though these voices aren't loud,
they're loud enough, listen; the closet door
itself is calling you, the evening star
you hid inside that closet and the cloud
you buried underneath a closet floor—
they're calling you to be the man you are.

IN THE PARK AS DAY RETREATS

As day retreats and twilight falls, let night
begin. Beneath tall trees one shadow calls
his comrades to emerge as twilight falls,
as day retreats and snatches up the light
it left behind. The empty park, once bright
with sunshine, fills with shadows; darkness crawls
across the sky, collapsing closet walls,
shelves, doors, while redefining black and white.

More and more shadows gather here as day
retreats, as twilight falls. Although it's dark,
I can detect the presence of a thin,
pale crescent moon that won't consent to stay
much longer in its closet; in this park
let night begin at last, let night begin.

MIRACLE IN BROAD DAYLIGHT

Today two men were walking down the street.
Their age was twenty-five or so; and they
were walking hand in hand. At noon. Today
I saw a miracle—let me repeat
the facts: two men were not ashamed to greet
the world without a mask, nor did they pay
attention to foul words the world might say;
and yet the ground stayed calm beneath their feet.

There was no earthquake, nor a savage flood.
No fire and brimstone falling from the sky.
No serpents biting heels. I ask myself
what time is it and write this with my blood:
two men are walking hand in hand, while I
am in a shoebox on a closet shelf.

THE MANNEQUIN

Deception is a complicated skill,
more intricate than making violins
or frescoing a wall. We mannequins
must mimic men, for there's no magic pill
or medicine for us which would instill
virility and strength, no vitamins
to make us healthier or tiger-skins
which we could wear against the winter's chill.

Like all good mannequins, I spend my life
pretending I'm a "normal" man. And I
succeed quite well; I'm talented and smart
enough to wield a surgeon's sterile knife,
removing "f" from life to form a lie
that no one can detect—I've learned the art.

SOMEWHERE

Somewhere there's truth. Somewhere a closet door
has opened. Somewhere shadows write their name
on calling cards without a sense of shame
or guilt. Somewhere these shadows do not store
white lies on closet shelves; instead they're sure
their dice have not been rigged and so don't blame
the die they roll but simply play the game
as best they can, no matter what the score.

Somewhere a man like me can tell his wife
he's gay. Somewhere a man like me removes
his mask. Somewhere a man like me can share
his feelings with his children, share his life,
his twilight and his night. Such candor proves
no matter win or lose, there's truth somewhere.

AFTER

after the rope has snapped   after the fall
        after the iron ladder you've tried to climb
collapses with a crash   after your rhyme
no longer rhymes   after your closet's wall
begins to crack   after shadows who call
your name forget your name   perhaps it's time
for you to pay the quarter or the dime
it costs to see if you can love at all

perhaps it's time to face the truth   to face
a mirror and behold your face without
a mask   perhaps it's time to understand
it's not too late to deal yourself an ace
of hearts and king of spades   after the drought
perhaps it's time to water desert sand

CLOSET ARITHMETIC

Behind the closet door you calculate,
subtract and add your shadows' numbers: two
plus one is sometimes less than three as you
relearn addition and subtraction—eight
plus four is sometimes more than twelve, what's straight
is sometimes circular, and what you knew
before is now irrelevant, since few
is sometimes many, little—sometimes great.

You have discovered seven minus six
is sometimes less than one, that nine plus three
is sometimes more than twelve, that four times four
is sometimes seventeen. Arithmetic's
new axioms enable you to see
how more is sometimes less, and less is more.

BRAVERY

Last week one student stood before our school
and told us all he's gay. He stood before
the principal and teachers on a shore
where Grecian sailors built a horse to fool
the troops of Troy who used to ridicule
the Greeks. The Trojans thought they should ignore
forbidden dreams, like his, or could implore
the gods of Troy to keep out Greek misrule.

I'm jealous of his bravery—a boy
of seventeen or eighteen doesn't fear
to tell the truth, while I, much closer to
his father's age, am frightened men of Troy
will rise up from their graves with sword and spear
if I acknowledge what I know is true.

THINGS GET LOST

Things get lost: gloves. A sock. A fork. A spoon.
Receipts you need. A bill you have to pay.
Your birth certificate. The month of May.
A language you once spoke. The month of June.
A certain man you loved; the afternoon
you met him and the night he walked away.
His name. His voice. The prayers you used to pray.
High tides that flow according to the moon.

Things get lost: jungles. Seas. The planet Mars.
Photos of your kids. Birthday cards your wife
had given you and which you used to give
your wife as well. Your wedding ring. Thick bars
on prison windows. Closet doors. The life
you could have lived. The truth. The life you live.

MISPLACED

It's easy to misplace a key—and snow
from the South Pole and ice from Hudson Bay.
By sheer bad luck you can misplace the day
that you were born. Self-portraits by Van Gogh,
the White House and a herd of buffalo
may also be misplaced. Some shadows say
they once misplaced the city of Calais,
while others claim the city was Bordeaux.

It's easy to misplace a scarf. A shoe.
A hat. A dream. And Lake Ontario
or islands like New Guinea and Zanzibar
might be misplaced if you're not careful, too.
I thought that I am careful; what happens, though,
when you misplace the man you really are?

CLOSET #4: 1990-1999

BREAKFAST TABLE

I'm eating with my wife and children by
our sunny kitchen table, sitting where
I always sit, when suddenly I hear
a pounding on the closet door. I sigh,
but clearly hear a banging and the cry
of shadows loudly shouting they will tear
the door to pieces, terrified with fear
of slowly choking, frightened they will die.

*"We're suffocating in the closet, life
 is leaving us!"* My younger son now feeds
the cat. His older brother wants to see
a movie at the mall, and tells my wife
he won't be home till late. My daughter reads
a book. The only one who hears is me.

DICHOTOMY

This is my Day-life. Sitting with my wife
and children by the breakfast table, I
close the curtains, afraid a passerby
might stop to gape at us. I take a knife
and butter the children's bread. STRIP. STRAP. STRIFE.
Neighbors say, *"Such a good husband"* (a lie
of course), *"and such a good father too"* (I sigh
of course). During the day this is my life.

This is my Night-life. Shadows first unglue
me from my chair, and after they untie
my hands, I board a rocketship to Mars.
Upon arrival, Martians take me to
a beach. *"Look up,"* they say, *"look at the sky."*
This is my Night-life: galaxies of stars.

THE MARTIAN

What planet are you from? Are you from Mars
like me? We Martians find it very hard
to feel at home on Earth, a planet marred
by animosity to other stars,
to men from other worlds. An Earthling gnars
when we embrace; the love a Martian bard
will sing about most Earthlings disregard.
They laugh at us and mock our Martian scars.

Although these Earthlings frequently assert
we Martians are unwanted immigrants,
my telescope detects on Earth a man—
a human male—he's taking off his shirt—
his undershirt—his pants—his underpants—
I race to Earth as quickly as I can.

WELCOME TO MARS

Welcome to Mars. Here is our Martian bed
which you and I will fill with Martian rust,
the product of our iron, rain and lust.
Let me caress your shoulders, neck and head,
your chest, your back, your arms, your legs. How red
you are—the Martian midday sunlight must
have burned your skin. We Martians shouldn't trust
the sun, but bow before our moons instead.

The moment that you leave your closet, there
is Deimos, there is Dread. The moment that
you leave your closet, Phobos, too, unbars
himself, releasing Fear. Both Dread and Fear
accompany us Martians, staring at
a ruddy sky. Welcome, welcome to Mars.

EXPLORING MARS

Earth's scientists, believing there's no sea
on Mars, insist the planet is as dry
as Mercury. They haven't seen what I
have seen: beneath red desert scenery,
an ocean flows. And there's a colony
of mermen in that sea who do not cry
about their lack of legs but simply try
to live a life of aquatic dignity.

Beneath the arid surface, mermen are
as free as dolphins back on Earth, as free
as shadows who have managed to unlock
their closet's door and leave the door ajar.
And in my dreams, these mermen flock to me
to show me where my rocketship can dock.

SPEAKING MARTIAN

In Martian, every verb must end with "y,"
while nouns must end with "o," or rhyme with "o:"
amigo, scorpio, camerado.
So many words are new: to merman-try,
to twilight-stay, to closet-nullify.
And old words have new meanings: shadow—glow—
Its most unique, distinctive feature, though,
is Martian syntax doesn't let you lie.

In Martian, you must tell the truth, without
the luxury of swimming in a sea
of falsehoods or of using words as masks.
It doesn't matter if you whisper, shout
or cry—you have to answer truthfully
the complex questions which a Martian asks.

TRANSLATING MARTIAN

Translation is a skill all Martians learn;
on Mars, a "closet" means a passageway
that leads you to the inlet of a bay
where mermen play a game of tag. "To yearn"
refers to watching distant campfires burn
while drifting on a raft. In Martian, "day"
is when a closet-merman has to stay
ashore while waiting for the tide to turn.

We sometimes translate "gay" as "happy" but
its meaning can be "sad," depending on
the ebbing of the tides. The hardest word
to translate is the simplest—"love," we shut
the covers of our Martian lexicon,
our glasses lost at sea, our vision blurred.

INTRODUCTION TO MARS

When you were still a boy, you didn't know
too much about the planet Mars—a dead,
abandoned world without a sea; instead
of fertile Earth, you'd find a wasteland, so
you thought. Its rusty deserts couldn't grow
a single plant, just like its moons of Dread
and Fear; according to the books you read,
all signs of life had vanished long ago.

But now you know this isn't true. You're not
a little boy, you've learned there's oxygen
on Mars to fill your lungs, and rain, and dew.
You've learned that Mars has jungles, humid, hot
and green. That Mars has blue lagoons. That men
can live on Mars. That you're a Martian, too.

NUMBERS

What happens when you sense you're drawn to men?
You count these men—*one, two, three, four*—but run
away from them; you run in hope that none
of them will ever overtake you, then
you turn around and stop, in hope that when
they spot you, they'll try to lasso you or stun
you with a laser. You start counting: *one,*
two, three, four, five, six, seven, eight, nine, ten.

You imagine counting numbers—*one, two,*
three, four—may somehow cause your closet walls
to split. Perhaps you're really counting bars
that you will visit and the benches you
will sit upon in parks when twilight falls,
or maybe grains of sand you'll find on Mars.

FREE ASSOCIATION

You hear a certain word and then you say
whatever it evokes. The first word—night:
a closet's moon. *The moon*: the mirrored light
a shadows sees. *A closet*: where I play
my silent flute. *A shadow*: someone gay
who tries to hide his flute of truth. *Stage fright*:
when flutes are played at noon. *The truth*: a flight
to Mars. *A poem*: a prayer some shadows pray.

The planet Mars: a place where men like me
feel free enough to throw away their masks.
Marriage: we look into a looking-glass,
my wife and I, but I don't let her see
my shadow there. *A prayer*: a shadow asks
for three dimensions, depth, some weight and mass.

THE GAY BAR

I stood before its door but was afraid
to enter, frightened if I entered I
would cross night's Rubicon, or maybe fly
to Mars and not return to Earth, or wade
into a whirlpool, having now betrayed
my wife. Just as fainthearted lions lie
in waiting, so I stood there, waiting; by
and by I left, although my shadow stayed.

My shadow stayed and still it stays there, like
a lion waiting for its prey—it waits
but can't decide exactly what to do.
How long until it feels it's time to strike,
how long? It hesitates and hesitates
and hesitates till all my lies come true.

ENLOCKED

you're not allowed to touch the lock   you're not
allowed to hope you're strong enough to break
the cage   you're not allowed to even shake
its bars   you're not allowed to wonder what
it's like to cruise aboard a yawl   a yacht
a skiff   you're not allowed to stay awake
all night imagining brave sailors take
you to an island tropical and hot

you're not allowed to burn when standing near
another man who burns   you're not allowed
to sparkle in the dark   or glow   or gleam
you're not allowed to breathe the atmosphere
of Mars or fantasize a Martian cloud
embraces you   you're not allowed to dream

52

HOW

How tides in the ocean of my closet rise
and fall—how mermen in my closet's sea
swim closer to the shore, inviting me
to join them—how a friendly shadow tries
invoking Mars each time I close my eyes—
how my children's father can also be
a Martian—how I lost the recipe
for truth-soup—how I catalogue my lies—

how I hear the banjo a Martian strums—
how fallen stars may sometimes incandesce
and glow behind a closet door—how now
becomes tomorrow, a day that never comes
except on Martian soil—do I possess
enough courage to tell my children *how*?

REMEMBRANCE OF THINGS PAST

Forget the rules. Forget the laws. Forget
your parents' expectations and the kind
of life your parents live. Forget the blind,
the deaf, the mute, the lame. Forget the debt
you owe your teachers and the alphabet
you learned. Forget the banker's check you signed
which can't be cashed, and linen intertwined
with woolen threads. Forget your silhouette.

Remember what you saw on Mars: how green
a Martian forest really is, how blue
a Martian sea. Remember, too, the stars
that dot the Martian heavens aren't seen
on Earth. Remember Martian songbirds you
have heard. Forget the Earth. Remember Mars.

CIRCLING MARS

Aboard a spaceship circling Mars, I see
the living body of the planet: seas,
high mountain peaks, polar glaciers that freeze
in winter and thaw in spring, tree after tree
in jungles and rainforests. Quietly
and unobtrusively, a gentle breeze
now pushes clouds aside; as if to please
me, Mars exposes himself, enticing me.

Back on Earth, I was taught that Mars is dead.
But look—Martians have built cities that glow
at night across the Martian plains, like stars
that twinkle on the surface, ruby red,
each city gleaming, glittering. But I know
only from outer space will I see Mars.

SOLAR SYSTEM

The men of Jupiter disdain the men
of Mars. Though they acknowledge Martian men
are males, these Martians aren't full-blown men,
according to the Jovians; "*true men
must dream of reaching Venus*," claim the men
of Jupiter, "*whereas the so-called men
of Mars know only sterile rust—and men
who live in barren deserts aren't men.*"

Between the planets Jupiter and Mars,
small asteroids revolve around the sun.
Because I live on one of them, I see
what Jovians don't see—I see that Mars
is green with meadows, blue with lakes, the sun
and Earth reflected in a Martian sea.

MARTIAN MUSIC

I wonder if the music that we'd find
on Mars is similar to music here
on Earth. I wonder if the music there
is something I'd enjoy—or if I'd mind
the fact its scale would be a different kind
of scale. I think most Earthlings wouldn't care
for Martian music, but in dreams I share
with shadows there's a music-box I wind.

Emerging from this music-box there seems
to be a tune I would have heard if I
had climbed aboard a rocketship to Mars
when I was young. But now I'm old—my dreams
don't have a sound-track and the closet sky
I see is overcast, devoid of stars.

DO MARTIANS DREAM?

Do Martians dream about the life they might
have lived if they had stayed on Earth, if they
had missed the rocketship that flew away
to Mars? From what I've read, the Martian night
is sometimes very dark, without the light
reflected by Earth's moon, so Martians may
believe because the Earth is different, day
and night on Earth are luminous and bright.

Yet even if a Martian dreams about
the life he doesn't live on Earth, I think
he knows he lives a life of truth—a life
without the lies I tell myself, without
the table full of lies I eat and drink,
without the midnight lies I tell my wife.

LUCKY STARS

I thank my lucky stars my wife can't read
my thoughts. I thank my very lucky stars
she doesn't see the heavy prison bars
I bang my head against; she doesn't need
to know about the double life I lead:
one life on Earth with her, one life on Mars
with Martians playing banjos and guitars
to celebrate the day when Mars is freed.

One nightmare, though, invades my dreams; I try
to jail it but it keeps on strangling me:
one night my wife and I are on the lawn,
we're making love, I look up at the sky
—and all the stars are gone; my wife can see
my thoughts, and all my lucky stars are gone.

INCANTATION

"Hocus pocus mini mocus: create
another universe to parallel
our present one"—recite this magic spell
and presto!—Martian streams will irrigate
the fields of Mars as Martians celebrate
prosperity. They'll also find the well
they've dug has overflowed; its waters swell
and inundate the dunes of Martian fate.

All former shadows here on Earth are free
to sunbathe all day long; they need not shut
a closet door or lie about the life
true mermen lead while swimming in the sea.
A universe like this is magic—but—
but what about my children and my wife?

THE CLOSET LIBRARY

When browsing in the Closet Library,
you come across uncensored books you will
not find in other places—for example,
"The Shadow from Seville." Although the sea
is far away, the hero dreams that he
has found a merman in his closet till
he learns it is the Shadow from Seville,
who helps the hero find some dignity.

Pick up "The Martian Sonnets," where you'll find
two hundred sonnets, all describing life
on Mars. Or take "The Looking-Glass," which seems
to mirror truth. The closet walls are lined
with books for you to borrow, books your wife
will probably never read—just like your dreams.

THE LOOKING-GLASS

Here is a mirror. Look carefully, you'll find
yourself, of course, but if you look again,
you'll notice shadows from your closet, men
from Mars who live on Earth, and right behind
the Martians, mermen who can read your mind.
Look in the mirror. Gaze at the future, when
your closet door will open and the pen
you hold rewrites what censors underlined.

Here is a ladder. Hold it with all your might
and climb into the mirror. Good. Don't ask
too many questions. Under the glass you'll see
a figure in a costume standing right
behind the mermen. Throw away his mask.
Shout your name. Maybe—maybe—you'll be free.

MODESTY

THEY shake their heads and say that modesty
forbids me from describing what I keep
inside my closet or how shadows sleep
with one another, thigh by thigh. THEY see
the pages I have written, and decree
I must exterminate all words that creep
like lice along the body and then leap
like fleas from head to head immodestly.

"But what about the truth?" I answer THEM.
"Like body lice, like fleas, the truth is God's
creation so it also has the right
to live." THEY sit in judgment and condemn
the truth to freeze to death; what are the odds
it will survive without some warmth or light?

THE SPECIMEN

Be quiet, very quiet when THEY start
to talk about the bolted closet where
we dwell. It's all a clever ruse to snare
you if you start to stutter, for THEY'RE smart
enough to grasp your stammer means you're part
and parcel of our blood. And THEY won't spare
you once THEY catch you, once THEIR scalpels tear
your arteries as THEY dissect your heart.

Be quiet then, be very quiet when
THEY start a conversation and THEY speak
about our closet or the shadows who
inhabit it. THEY need a specimen
whose backbone has collapsed to prove how weak
we shadows are; that specimen is you.

SHUT THE CLOSET DOOR

"Shut it, shut it quickly," THEY order me,
"and also lock it, lock the closet door,
then promptly throw away the key before
a shadow can escape, before he'll see
he's trapped inside tonight, no longer free
to enter dreams, to touch your bed, to pour
you cups of wine, to wander past the shore
where mermen swim, to plant another tree."

"Stand straight," THEY yell, *"and place your hands beside*
your thighs, we'll wrap tight swaddling clothes around
your body and your head." THEY whisper, *"Good,*
quite good," when THEY behold me mummified,
my legs, my hands, my mouth completely bound.
"You're perfect now, you look the way you should."

ACCEPTANCE

THEY don't accept I've witnessed Martian rain.
THEY don't accept a man from Earth has been
to Mars where there's sufficient oxygen
to breathe, sufficient CO_2 for grain.
THEY don't accept a Martian may disdain
the dictionaries THEY compile, for in
THEIR language, "mask" means "truth," "affection"—"sin,"
and "Martian love," a synonym for "pain."

THEY don't accept the fact my closet has
a launching pad for rocketships that fly
to planets far beyond THEIR prison bars
and reach a Martian sea as boundless as
the seas on Earth. THEY don't accept that I
can bring THEM proof there's really life on Mars.

ABOMINATION

Yes, THEY detest true Martians, THEY deplore
freed mermen, THEY abhor the shadow in
my twilight's closet who emerges thin
and hungry, begging me to leave the door
ajar and smuggle in some bread before
he starves to death. THEY claim it is a sin
for him to eat, and much to his chagrin,
demand I shouldn't feed him anymore.

THEY tell me it's abominable to bow
before wild mermen, that it's wrong to till
the soil of Mars. But if I've ever prayed,
the shadow in my closet taught me how
to pray, to bend my will before the will
of God and to accept the way we're made.

PROHIBITED

THEY ought to set up billboards here and write
the things THEY claim we're not supposed to do—
*PROHIBITED: TO PADDLE A CANOE
ACROSS A MARTIAN LAKE; TO DYNAMITE
A CLOSET DOOR; TO HOLD A PLEBISCITE
ON LETTING MARTIANS SPEAK THE TRUTH; TO VIEW
THE SEA ON MARS AT DUSK; TO DREAM OF YOU;
PROHIBITED: TO DREAM OF YOU TONIGHT.*

*THE SUN: PROHIBITED; THE MOON AND STARS:
PROHIBITED; A ROCKETSHIP ABOVE
EARTH'S ATMOSPHERE: PROHIBITED; A BREATH
OF MARTIAN AIR ATOP THE CLIFFS OF MARS:
PROHIBITED; TO SHOUT IT'S YOU I LOVE:
PROHIBITED, BY PENALTY OF DEATH.*

PERCUSSION

I listen to THEIR drumming every day;
yet even so, I do not understand
the reason for THEIR pounding rhythm and
the loudness of THEIR drums. I wish that THEY
would choose a different instrument and play
the soft, melodic music which a band
of fiddlers play; I wish a harpist's hand
would wave and make the drummers go away.

To be quite honest, though, the silence of
the shadows in my closet is the kind
of music I appreciate as well—
I listen to the shadows' dreams of love,
to soundless dreams which echo in the mind
without xylophone or gong or bell.

THE PENITENTIARY

A sonnet is a closet with a key
that's capable of opening the door
which THEY have bolted, locked and barred. *"Ignore
all meter and all rhyme,"* THEY shout at me,
*"why don't you run away, why don't you flee
the sonnet prison with its concrete floor
as cold as ice, its dungeon walls where more
is less, its narrow cells of prosody?"*

I shake my head. "The minute that you find
the closet key, the man you might have been
becomes the man you are, at liberty
to stroll amidst wild orchids of the mind
in meadows of the metaphor. For in
the sonnet / closet / theater, you are free."

DISAPPROVAL

THEY disapprove of everything I say.
THEY disapprove of everything I think
defines the essence of my life: the link
connecting mermen to the interplay
of words. THEY disapprove each time I stay
too long along the shore where mermen drink
and eat; THEY disapprove of purple ink
which THEY insist I need to throw away.

When I unlocked my closet door, THEY hissed
and booed, for THEY condemned my swimming with
a merman in the eddies of the sea
that I discovered there. Yet THEY insist
a merman can't exist, that he's a myth.
My biggest problem, though, is THEY are me.

INDEPENDENCE DAY

Today is mine, not THEIRS; this room is mine,
this table and this chair is mine; the sky
outside the window, too, is mine. And I
am free to write these words, am free to sign
my name beneath them and to underline
the whitest ones. Although THEY might deny
I've written this or may attempt to dye
the whiteness of these words, these words will shine.

These lines are mine, not THEIRS, these lines of where
I need to go, of what I need to do,
of when, of why, of how. You laugh; you say
my life is THEIRS, not mine, you say I fear
the sky will fall if I spell out just who
I am. Perhaps you're right—but not today.

THE PURPLE MOCKINGBIRD

Inside my cage, there is a mockingbird
I need to strangle with my hands. I fear
that if the cage's door unbolts, he'll share
the secrets of my heart—the secret word,
the secret deed—with parrots, with a herd
of cows, with snakes, with apes, with every bear
he'll meet, with every stallion, colt and mare,
with every creature: feathered, scaled or furred.

Oh if this purple bird escapes, he'll sing
about the naked shadows I concealed
behind a closet door, he'll give a voice
to them. And if he does, then everything
I've tried to hide for years will be revealed.
I have to kill the bird. I have no choice.

PERCEPTION

If everyone was deaf, and only you
could hear, could anything you write explain
what thunder is   the pounding of the rain
how roosters crow, hens cluck, sheep bleat, cows moo?
If everyone was blind and had no clue
what color is, but you could see a train
painted pink or a purple weather-vane,
could you explain what yellow is? red? blue?

My wife is straight. My children, too, are straight.
My neighbors and the people who I pray
with all are straight. They neither hear nor see
shadows dancing in my closet who wait
for dusk to fall   the Martian stowaway
or mermen from Atlantis calling me.

CLOSET #5: 2000-2009

AGE 50

He's young, he's only twenty-four, I'm old
enough to be his father but I dream
I'm twenty-four again. Around us steam
is rising from the jungle floor; no cold
can overcome our heat as we behold
a fiery jungle sun. We find a stream
where we may bathe together for I gleam
and glisten when I touch his youthful gold.

Awake, I know he shouldn't sacrifice
his youth for me, I know he shouldn't swim
in arctic seas. Behind my closet door
my ocean's filled with icebergs whose thick ice
will never melt. Why do I dream of him?
He's very young, he's only twenty-four.

OLD ENOUGH

You're old enough to know you mustn't flirt
with younger men. You're old enough to know
you mustn't let your mask fall down, or show
a stranger's eye the hair beneath your shirt.
You're old enough to know you mustn't hurt
your children or your wife; let rivers flow
inside your closet, let a tempest blow
there too, but let your wife preserve her skirt.

You're old enough to know you mustn't hold
the hand another man extends to you,
or wear his gloves, their leather coarse and rough,
although they fit you perfectly. You're old
enough to know your children's eyes pursue
you everywhere you go. You're old enough.

WILD ORCHIDS

I know I'll never sleep with you. I know
I'll never pluck your rose or even touch
its stem. I know you'll never know how much
your fragrance fills my dreams. I'll never show
you scarlet jungles where my orchids grow,
wild orchids no one picks but me. I clutch
them now, the way men clutch at twigs on such
a night like this, when rivers overflow.

I have a wife I married years ago,
before you bloomed. We raised our children well.
With warmth. I think my family loves me, too.
I write on petals so that winds will blow
these words away for good; I'll never tell
you face-to-face it's you I love, it's you.

TABOO

I mustn't utter phrases like "*it's you
I love, it's you;*" I'm not allowed to say
such words because such words are banned today,
tomorrow, and as long as red and blue
make purple or as long as two plus two
make four. Perhaps if red and blue made gray
or two plus two made three, I'd find a way
to liberate what now remains taboo.

I can't release imprisoned words which lie
below my closet's floor, I can't unsheathe
a sword to rip apart this floor and free
the shackled truth; the only place where I
can say "*it's you I love*" is underneath
the corals of my closet's silent sea.

SHARING

It's absolutely clear to me, as plain
as bread, there is no possibility
I'll ever share my life with you. I see
my wine is liquor you won't touch, my grain
is wheat which you're allergic to; in vain
I've hoped that you could share your meals with me.
But surely there are other things which we
might somehow share, like thunder, or the rain.

So many things to share: the sky; the air;
this wind which strokes my cheek may stroke the fuzz
upon your cheek as well; a cloud; a bird.
What does it matter if we'll never share
a bed, a kiss or an embrace? What does
it matter if we'll never share a word?

LUCK

How fortunate we are, the language that
I write in is the language that you speak.
So we have words to share: Wing. Feather. Beak.
Nest. Branch. The cat I saw—is it the cat
you saw as well? And what about the rat
I'm frightened of? This year, this month, this week
are also things we share, just like the streak
of sunset orange we've both been staring at.

The chair on which I sit, was that your chair?
The sea in which I swim, is it the sea
you swam in, too? How fortunate we are,
that we can share a sea, that we can share
a thing as intimate as chairs, that we
can share a train. A bus. A trolley car.

BRIGHT STAR

There is a star of honesty—Bright Light!
Enraptured by its shine and brilliancy,
I dream of grabbing it, for it would free
me from my lies. A man who's lucky might
be fortunate enough to have his night
enlightened by this star of honesty.
You'd see it too, if you'd look up like me;
you have, in fact, a better sense of sight.

I dare not tell you that I dream of men—
of men like you—of you, damn you. And this
condemns me to behold that glow of white
grow dimmer week by week. I grab a pen
and write this down while there's still light—there is
a star of honesty, no longer bright.

THE SURF

I am afraid to touch you with my hand;
instead, I'll touch you with the words I write,
with images of ocean waves at night,
the footprints of a seagull on the sand,
a crescent moon. I hope you'll understand
the breeze that touches you is mine, the light
a lighthouse flashes you is mine, the white
and shadowed clouds, the air, the sea, the land.

I hope that you will understand how much
I want to touch you, here and now, embrace
you, here and now. Take the shore, take the brine,
they're yours. I hope the words I write will touch
you in the dark, will stroke your arms, your face,
will press your body nearer, close to mine.

EPISTLE

Only now, in the covert of the night,
my wife asleep beside me, can I turn
to you in writing, hoping you may learn
that I exist. Despite the darkness, light
emerges from an inner closet, bright
enough to write by. Star by moon I yearn
for you, my camerado; though I burn
these pages every morning, still I write.

How would my wife react if shadows stood
beside our bed and showed her where I hide
these words before they're burned? What would she think
if she discovered them? And you—what would
you do with them as well? Would you decide
to burn these words I write in closet-ink?

COMMUNICATION

I do not tell you what to do or what
you're not supposed to do. I do not tell
you how to spell your name or not to spell
your name—or when to read a book or not
to read a book in Greek—or where you've got
to go or where you shouldn't go—which well
to drink from when you're thirsty, or which bell
to ring when doors are locked and days are hot.

I do not talk to you. Instead, I write
you letters, since the possibility
of speaking face-to-face and telling you
to come is almost nil. I tell the night,
however, I have dreamt you talk to me
from dawn to dusk of things we ought to do.

CONSIDERATION

I have a daughter and a son. Because
I have my children to consider, I
cannot consider you. My children cry
at night, for in their dreams, huge monster-jaws
are seen emerging from the sea; the maws
of giant sharks then open wide and try
to swallow them alive. But by-and-by
I comfort them, until the sea withdraws.

I have my wife as well, who's very kind
to me and to my daughter and my son,
small fragile rafts that drift upon the sea
I've made. I must remove you from my mind,
I have to make believe your boat has gone
away for good—its anchor, lost—like me.

CORONATION

The shadows in my closet crowned me king
of liars for I lie not only to
my wife, my friends, my children and to you,
but even to myself—there's not a thing
I say that echoes truth. The royal ring
I wear is counterfeit, the revenue
my court receives is not the homage due
an honest king, but driftwood shadows bring.

My kingdom is a closet filled with lies;
seaweeds are my crown; palaces I own
are made from sand and shells, which oceans might
engulf and wash away. I fantasize
each morning I would abdicate my throne
if I could hold your scepter just one night.

SUPPOSED TO

So many things I'm not supposed to do:
I'm not supposed to gather seashells or
bits of coral behind a closet door,
or look at seagulls, flying two by two.
I'm not supposed to notice just how blue
a closet ocean is, or go explore
its depths, or try to map the ocean floor;
I'm not supposed to dive for pearls with you.

I'm not supposed to swim with you, or think
it's somehow possible that you and I
could share a sea together, free at last.
I'm not supposed to take a pen and ink
and write the truth; I'm just supposed to lie
about the ocean: boundless, endless, vast.

WHERE

Tell me, where am I?—and you—where are you?
Where is the sea whose waves we heard, the sea
in which we could have swum, the ocean we
ignored? Where is the white seagull that flew
from my dreams to yours? Where is the tree that grew
and flourished on the beach's sand, the tree
we dared not climb? Where is the memory
of summer dawn we never shared or knew?

Tell me, where is the sun that could have shone
if we had let it shine? Where is our youth,
the youth we threw away? Where is the sky
whose clouds we could have touched if we had flown
the plane we never flew, the plane of truth?
Tell me, where are you?—and I—where am I?

THE FOLLOWER

I am your shadow, so wherever you go,
I go—be it in taxis, buses, cars,
I follow you. I use binoculars
and telescopes to follow you, and though
you may not see me, and may not even know
I am your shadow, I follow you to Mars,
to Cassiopeia's chair, to unnamed stars
whose light is yours, where even shadows glow.

I'm your shadow. You may not see me but
wherever you go, I go, I touch your skin,
I touch your luster and your sheen, I see
you gleaming in the closet's night sky. Shut
the door. Stretch out your hand and touch me in
the dark. I am your shadow. Look at me.

LAVA

I love you, but I'm careful no one hears
my thoughts. I love you, but you'll never hear
me say these words. Although I might appear
to be a frozen lake, beneath veneers
of ice a sea of lava reappears
all set to burst fire on fire, yet I share
my sealed volcano with no one, for fear
it could ignite a dozen atmospheres.

I close my eyes and make believe we are
together, you and I, a dozen stars
from here. I make believe we both take part
in building rocketships to reach that star,
for there, beyond both Jupiter and Mars,
we love, body to body, heart to heart.

74

TIERRA DEL FUEGO

Because I burst with fire, I wanted snow
to avalanche my mind, I wanted cold
to turn my body into ice. I told
the wind to bring a hailstorm and to blow
as harshly as it could because I know
that fire can burn as lava, uncontrolled
and wild; I've seen erupting flames enfold
a mountain peak and make its summit glow.

I feared volcanoes, hoping I might freeze
the magma in my heart, preventing heat
from swelling up and scorching every tree
I've ever planted or from broiling seas.
But how could I foresee that I would meet
you? Look—my ice is melting, drowning me.

SNOWMAN

Don't stand so close, don't look at me that way,
don't stretch your hand towards mine. I am a man
who needs the frost of winter rather than
the April warmth you offer me. Don't say
my name, don't say a single word, your May
is stronger than December sleet—how can
I hope to freeze when everything I plan
to petrify will flower if you stay.

I am afraid that if you stay with me
a little longer all my ice will start
to melt, returning birds will want to sing,
and buds begin appearing on my tree.
I am afraid the winter will depart,
I am afraid your touch will herald spring.

SPRING

Some snowmen argue spring exists; when spring
arrives at last, all snow will go away
and ice will melt. These snowmen even say
that spring permits a mute like me to sing
out loud and drown out howling storms which bring
us sheets of hail. The sky, no longer gray,
becomes a vibrant, brilliant blue as May
begins to reign as queen, and June as king.

No winter lasts forever, snowmen claim;
the cold will disappear and I'll be free
to light a fire—I've never known a fire,
is it as green as spring? I'll have a name
as well, for spring permits a mute like me
to have a name as verdant as desire.

BENEATH THE BALCONY

You do not see me in the darkness for
you're standing in a room whose chandelier
is radiant with light. I do not dare
move closer when I spot you by a door
which opens to the balcony. I swore
I wouldn't stare at you again, yet here
I am—as weak as perjurers who swear
they will not smoke tobacco anymore.

I see you looking out the window at
the darkness, but the darkness doesn't let
you see me gazing up at you. The night
is kind, preventing you from seeing that
it's you I love—for you're the cigarette
I mustn't smoke, I mustn't even light.

WONDERMAN

I wonder if you stare at what I stare.
I wonder if you walk upon the sand
I walk upon. I wonder if the band
that plays my music is the band you hear
as well. I wonder if you breathe the air
I breathe. I wonder if you understand
the language that I speak, its grammar and
its words, or if you fear the fears I fear.

I wonder if you open closet doors.
I wonder if you enter closets, too.
I wonder if you see the sea I see
—a closet's sea—and map its different shores.
I wonder if you know I dream of you.
I wonder if you ever dream of me.

NOT HERE, NOT NOW

I dare not sing a song with you—not here,
not now; I dare not dance a dance with you
—not here, not now. I dare not wear the shoe
you wear, the hat you wear, the shirt you wear;
I dare not look at how you look, I dare
not stare—not here, not now. I dare not do
the things you do: grab the sun, rendezvous
with stars; I dare not bear the light you bare.

I dare not touch the clouds you touch, the sky
you touch, the moon you touch. I dare not fly
to Mars the way you fly. I dare not bow
before the truth but neither will I lie
to you—not here, not now: if only I
could go embrace you, yes, right here, right now.

BETTER LEFT UNSAID

I've never seen you lying in a bed
asleep. I've never seen you with your eyes
shut tight amidst a dream that beautifies
you even more. I've never seen your head
upon a pillow or your legs outspread
beside a blanket tossed aside, your thighs
exposed, your body bared. I visualize
this often but it's better left unsaid.

It's better left unsaid because I know
there is no chance I'll ever see you in
a bed, especially my bed. There is
no chance because of Pan; I am too slow
to run away from him. I see Pan grin
at me—the only bed I'll share is his.

BEYOND THIS PARK

Beyond the twilight of this park, beyond
these benches where we sit, beyond this tree
whose branches cover us, there has to be
that paradise where fig-leaves we have donned
are stripped away; beyond this palm-tree's frond,
the word forbidden is forgotten, we
are free to love each other, we are free
beyond this hedge, these bushes and this pond.

You shake your head in disbelief, but I
believe that somewhere, there's abundant grace,
abundant light, where people will not curse
or mock us anymore; beyond the sky,
beyond the furthest stars, there's such a place
beyond this dusk, beyond this universe.

RIDING THE DRAGON

I'm not supposed to dream of you. I'm not
supposed to dream we're walking hand in hand
without our clothes upon a beach's sand.
The summer sky is cloudless, yet we spot
a darkish speck beyond the sun; the dot
becomes a winged dragon which will land
beside our feet. We climb its back, command
it to ascend and be our chariot.

While sitting on its back, I hold you tight.
We're rising now, above the beach, above
the sea, I'm holding you, I hear you say
my name, the turquoise sky is full of light,
you're holding me, the sky is full of love—
I'm not supposed to dream of you this way.

STORY HOUR

I've told the moon I dream of you—may she
begin emitting moonbeams causing you
to dream of me. I've told a comet to
appear as soon as evening falls—may he
start flashing, causing you to dream of me.
I've told the wind as well—a wind that blew
across a desert yet retained some dew
and mist. I've told each distant star I see.

I've told the shadows in my closet and
the mermen in my closet's seas I dream
of you. They listen, nod their heads and smile.
It's strange—the simple truth pulls back the hand
which covered both my eyes. It's strange—I seem
to see the heavens for a little while.

THE PEOPLE OF THE DAY

The People of the Day have other ways
of manifesting love; they do not stay
in closets, but they run outside to play
together, laughing all the while; they gaze
at one another openly for days
on end, not caring what the neighbors say.
I study them, the People of the Day,
as well as golden eggs their dragon lays.

For we, the shadows of the night, have much
to learn from them: the Man and Woman tamed
a dragon, allowing them to reach the sky.
Between its wings they lie and freely touch
each other, kiss, embrace; they're unashamed
to be in love and unashamed to fly.

THE NEGLECTED ORCHARD

Why do I feel ashamed to love, ashamed
to hold your hand in mine or call your name
out loud? Why do I feel a sense of shame
when I approach the orchard you have claimed
belongs to us, which others have defamed
as trees that bear no fruit? Must I disclaim
the right to love, admitting I'm to blame
for stunted, sterile trees that drought has maimed?

Why do I feel afraid to love, afraid
of what the neighbors think or what they'll say,
afraid to shout our orchard needs the rain
that surely would have fallen had I prayed
for rain to come; but I'm afraid to pray—
why must I be so rational and sane?

THE SCIENCE OF DESIRE

The science of desire is not precise;
it's hard to isolate and itemize
the colors of desire, then analyze
their properties and source. What triggers ice
to burn like coal? What makes men sacrifice
a wife when dazzling rainbows hypnotize
their eyes? What causes one to jeopardize
a marriage for a bowl of yellow rice?

Although the science of desire is not
exact, a researcher must not ignore
those factors that transform a frigid blue
to purple-pink, a pink which glows red-hot.
But look, I'm not objective anymore—
it's you that I desire, it's only you.

SPLINTER

I know I'm not supposed to want to touch
you in the dark. I know I'm not supposed
to want to touch you in the light, exposed
before the noonday sun. I know how much
more careful I must be, I know that such
a move by me would surely be opposed
by you. And all the love-poems I've composed
are merely splinters from a broken crutch.

I know I falter as I walk towards you.
I know I must withdraw my hand before
it reaches out. I even know you see
me as a pleasant fellow, someone who
is somewhat lame but pleasant—nothing more.
I fantasize you stretch your hand towards me.

IS THAT TOO MUCH

Is that too much to want, too much to ask,
too much to dream about at night, too much
to wish: that you'll extend one hand to touch
me while your other hand will hold a flask
of wine for us to drink? And yes, we'll bask
in sunshine afterwards. Right now I clutch
a mask I can't remove; I've heard there's such
a thing as hope; can hope remove a mask?

Is that too much to want: for prison gates
to open and the prisoner who sat
in darkness might look up? There, high above
him shines the sun   a sun that radiates
much warmth, much light. You are that sun. Is that
too much to want, to dream about: your love?

FOR YOU, AND ABOUT YOU

For you, and about you—this day, this night,
this week, month, year; something old, something new;
a coat, a scarf, a shoe that fits, a shoe
that doesn't fit, a shirt that is too tight
to wear, a shirt that is too loose; the sleight
of hand magicians need (which I need too
when I perform for you, and about you);
the flag of surrender, battles I must fight.

For you, and about you—the closet door,
the closet lock, the closet key, the sky
I sometimes see, the sky you also see.
For you, and about you—the books I tore,
pages I threw away, the hours I lie
in bed and wonder if you think of me.

CLOSET #6: 2010-2021

SILENCE

Silence then, only silence, not a word
about the orchids growing wild behind
my closet door, pink orchids of the mind;
and silence, too, about a mockingbird
with purple feathers and about that herd
of centaurs galloping since dawn to find
Apollo, unaware how he reclined
against a leafy vine, his speech all slurred.

Silence then, not a word to anyone
about the Cyclops underneath my bed
who wants to open all my closet's locks.
The moon, however, is not deaf; the sun
as well has overheard the words I said
to shadows trapped inside Pandora's box.

THE ENGLISH TEACHER

Today we'll read a poem by Robert Frost.
The speaker talks about a yellow wood
in which he came across two paths; how could
he choose the better one?   Perhaps he tossed
a coin. In any case, I also crossed
a fork like this when years ago I stood
before a choice. There was a man. A good,
courageous man. He is the path I lost.

Two roads. I took the asphalt one that led
me far away from him, I feared disgrace
and shame. Yet even now I can't erase
my memories of forest trails, the bed
we shared one night, his kisses and embrace,
his eager hands, his body and his face.

FAMILY MAN

Don't tell my children that I'm gay. Don't tell
them that I have a secret closet full
of shadows who stretch out their hands and pull
me in. Don't tell them how these shadows smell
a kindred spirit when I enter, spell
my name in Greek, and ask me to annul
the prohibition of linen mixed with wool;
don't tell them that their heaven is my hell.

Don't tell my wife how difficult it is
for me to sleep with her, don't tell her I
imagine she's a man I've met and make
believe her body isn't hers, but his.
Don't tell her when she falls asleep, I lie
awake and wait for shadows to awake.

THE PROFESSOR

My children and my wife believe I'm straight.
My students too believe the same, as do
my colleagues and the secretaries who
have worked with me for years. I educate
my pupils to pursue the truth and hate
hypocrisy, though possibly a few
of them may wonder whether I pursue
the truth when I step out the college gate.

When I take off the scholar's mask—when I
unpack my briefcase with its dozen books—
when I look in my bathroom mirror and
I see my closet's shadows standing by
my shoulders, how can I remove the hooks
from fish I've caught, all wriggling on the sand?

THE GRADUATE STUDENT

My student looks at me as if he knew.
He smiles a bit, as if he understood
I wish I were his age, I wish I could
be someone he might be attracted to.
He speaks to me as if he could unscrew
my closet door and analyze the wood
which lines my closet's walls; I see I should
be wary lest he find the beer I brew.

He senses that behind the cracked façade
of PhD and scholarship, I'm not
the staid professor I profess to be.
I have to be more circumspect. How odd
it is, the way his eyes precisely spot
the pocket where I keep my closet key.

MIRROR IN THE CLOSET

A mirror stands behind my closet door;
the closet's shadows hold it upright when
I try to throw it to the ground. But then
I stare at what I've seen, no longer sure
of what the mirror is reflecting or
revealing. Gazing back at me are men
who surface from my dreams; they've come again,
young men aged twenty three or twenty four.

I look once more and see myself—I'm old.
What happened to my spring, what happened to
my sunlit noon, what happened to my youth?
These men are younger than my sons. How cold
and dark it is, but what am I to do?
How cold it is, how dark it is, the truth.

THE SECRET GARDEN

The most essential thing, the inner core
of someone's life, is something no one knows
exists except for him. His secret grows
within a courtyard lacking gate or door,
a garden only he can enter or
unlock—as no one else may glimpse the rose
he cultivates, whose fragrance he'll disclose
to no one, no one, now or evermore.

He's cautious, fearful lest a stranger try
to pluck it, knowing how a flower dies
when touched, this flower he can't show or bring
to anyone at all—for he would die,
his garden sown with salt, if someone tries
uprooting it, the most essential thing.

COMPATRIOTS

The Swedes. The Swiss. The Serbs. The Portuguese.
The Welsh. The Dutch. The Czechs. The Catalans.
The French Canadians. The Mexicans.
The Falkland Islanders. The Japanese.
The Sri Lankans. The Thais. The Vietnamese.
The Kurds. The Yemenites. The Micronesians.
The Aborigines. The Eritreans.
The Zanzibari and the Congolese.

Among them all are closet-men who are
uncertain who they really are. Each one
of them will live his darkness or his light,
his desert or his sea, his map, his star.
Each neighbor, cousin, uncle, nephew, son.
My countrymen. My brothers of the night.

GRANDPA

I'm sixty-three. I made my choices long
ago—like locking closet doors at night
and plugging earplugs in my ears, in spite
of shadows who once argued I was strong
enough to smash down doors and hear the song
brave centaurs sang in praise of Athens' light
and Sparta's fire. But were my choices right
or wrong? What do I know of right and wrong?

I'm sixty-three. My grandson loves to play
with me, his sister brings me storybooks
to read to her—in English, not in Greek.
I chose to make believe I wasn't gay;
but was this choice correct? My grandson looks
for me—why not, I'm great at hide-and-seek.

WHO'S THERE?

Who's there? The drama of Prince Hamlet thus
begins. Perhaps our stories all begin
this way, mine too. *Who's there*? A shadow in
my bedroom closet, waiting for a bus
all day; an exiled Martian envious
of other Martians who have never been
displaced from Mars to Earth; a mannequin
who dreams of doing something scandalous.

Who's there? A merman in my closet's sea
who's searching for another merman who
might swim with him at night and doesn't fear
the dark. *Who's there*? The man I cannot be
except in words, a man who could unglue
the pages that I glued together here.

MY BEDROOM WALLS

Four silent Walls observe how I have lied
routinely to my wife, how straight lines curve
when she's not looking or the gall and nerve
I have when I declare that Truth has died.
These Walls observe how Truth must run inside
a closet when it's dark; four Walls observe
how closets I have painted black then serve
as air-raid shelters where poor Truth must hide.

My Walls observe Truth sometimes whispers, "Do
you hate me, friend?" I answer him, "Don't use
a word as harsh as hate, I love a bit
of Truth." My closet's shadows listen to
my words and can't believe their ears; they lose
their patience, "Liar! Coward! Hypocrite!"

THE TIME-BOMB

A time-bomb is now ticking—I'm not sure
exactly when it detonates: tonight,
tomorrow night, next week, next month. I fight
my fear and pray it won't explode before
I'm brave enough to break my closet door
and warn my wife and children; they have the right
to run for shelter when its dynamite
demolishes our home, from roof to floor.

I've tried, but there's no way to neutralize
the bomb; I hear it ticking all the time.
The bomb is in the chambers of my heart,
it's in my underpants, it's in my eyes:
I dream of undressed men, I dream that I'm—
the bomb will blow my family apart.

CENTAURS

Stop it, don't write another word, don't write
about the centaurs in your closet who
have galloped through your dreams. Stop now, if you
continue writing how the centaurs' night
illuminates your closet's dusk, you might
forget these words you've written could undo
you, words on twilight paper may pursue
you like freed centaurs racing towards the light.

Don't write another line. Your wife might find
a misplaced notebook, pick it up and read
it, page by page; how will you disavow
the evidence of hoof-prints in your mind?
If you're not careful, centaurs will stampede
across your marriage bed. Stop writing now.

OPENNESS

Open your heart and mind   Open your hand
to shake my hand   Open the books you close
Open each one of the closet walls, who knows
what you may find   perhaps a concert grand
piano   five harps   ten drums   perhaps a band
of jazz musicians   Open the sea that flows
all night   Open the wild orchid which grows
luxuriant amidst my closet's sand

Don't close the closet door again   Don't slam
it in my face   Don't shut the window, I
would like to breathe fresh air for once   Don't lock
the door and throw away the key, I am
a man like other men   Don't block the sky
Open your heart and mind, open your rock

91

THE ACCOUNTANT

I count the sudden thunderbolts which storm
my nights. I count the shadows who return
before the morning, asking me to yearn
for them the way they yearn for me; they swarm
around my pillow, hoping they'll transform
my dreams. I count Greek letters mermen learn
to read and write. I count the sticks I burn
to keep my fire aflame, to keep me warm.

I count the lies I tell, which may amount
to all the waves I've counted, waves that pound
the windswept beaches of my closet's sea.
And yet I must admit, I also count
my life a blessing since the day I found
that words are pearls my mermen bring to me.

SPELLING BEE

Let's start with ATTRACTION: *-s-t-o-p-*
Next word: NECESSARY: *-l-o-c-k-*
TRUTH: *-e-x-i-l-e-d-*   STOWAWAY:
-m-e-   JAILER: *-m-e-*   LIAR: *-m-e-*
YES: *-n-o-*   HOME: *-c-l-o-s-e-t-*
SHADOW: *-s-k-y-*   DESIRE: *-s-e-a-*
LOVE: *-h-o-p-e-l-e-s-s-*   GAY:
-p-r-o-h-i-b-i-t-e-d-

Let's continue with BROKEN: *-k-e-y-*
INTEGRITY: *-h-i-d-i-n-g-*
UNATTAINABLE: *-f-i-r-e-*   MEN:
-t-r-a-p-p-e-d-   ALIBI:
-e-v-e-n-i-n-g-   POETRY
-r-e-d-e-m-p-t-i-o-n-

REDEMPTION

the evening starts   but night will quickly end
a morning dawns   then afterwards, the noon
the afternoon   the dusk   and very soon
another night begins   the hours befriend
the weeks   the months   the years   bright stars ascend
to form ten thousand constellations strewn
beyond the sun, the planets and the moon
       so many mysteries to comprehend

and through it all, you're always haunted by
thin shadows in your closet   searching eyes
freed mermen in your dreams   forbidden lights
and through it all, your pen, with which you try
creating worlds   releasing earthbound skies
      redeeming cycles of these days, these nights

ALTERNATIVE

if you create another world beyond
this world, beyond the surf—if you create
another life beyond this life where fate
has more compassion for a vagabond
like you and won't demand you must respond
at once when officers interrogate
you on the beach and should you hesitate,
the deepest sea becomes a shallow pond—

if you can use imagination to
create a fellow swimmer who will give
you gifts of oceans that had only flowed
in dreams, a lover made of sand, of glue,
of waves, of wind—there is a chance you'll live,
there is a chance your time-bomb won't explode.

IN ORDER TO SURVIVE

In order to survive, you sometimes must
invent alternative realities:
the swimmer who will swim with you in seas
you share, and beaches where he lies, are just
mirages of imagination. Lust
of course is real, as real as twilight trees
in twilight parks with twilight canopies
whose twilight shadows rise from twilight dust.

You sometimes must invent alternative
realities, without the dust, without
the shadows or the trees. To feel alive,
to be alive, you sometimes have to give
yourself a lifeguard's megaphone and shout
you need a sea in order to survive.

RELEASE

When you admit the truth, a dam will break
as held-back yearnings, dreams, emotions flood
your valley, churning up a swell of mud;
yet all these surging, raging waters make
your desert bloom as well. The tranquil lake
behind the dam may disappear, but blood
will fill your veins when desert flowers bud
and blossom, and stark desert boulders quake.

When you admit the truth, a dam will burst
to sweep away your inhibitions and
allow you to be free, the driest heart
no longer dry. As water quenches thirst,
the truth will irrigate the waiting sand,
permitting you to plant the seeds of art.

A STRANGE DEVICE

There is a strange device allowing one
to slide from universe to universe
and reach a time and space that don't coerce
a person to belie the truth. The sun
is just as yellow there and stallions run
the same as here, but people do not nurse
a grudge against us shadow-men, nor curse
us for the things we've done or haven't done.

By using this device, a man like me
is able to explore a world beyond
his closet's ice, a world in which he's free
to build a submarine and cross a sea
far warmer than his closet's frozen pond.
This strange device is writing poetry.

STUCK

The closet door is stuck. The window, too,
won't budge an inch. How is a man like me
who cannot move the window shutters see
the world when there's so little he can view
from where he stands? And how can he pursue
the sun which must be shining somewhere he
has never been? Might sparks of honesty
reverse the darkness, changing false to true?

If there's no way to open up a door
or window, walk directly through a wall
in such a way that everything which clings
to them will disappear. No roof or floor
remains—you're in the air but do not fall,
for pages that you write on are your wings.

THE BERLIN WALL

I built a Berlin Wall to separate
two different men inhabiting my soul.
The West Berliner, cornflakes in his bowl,
seemed happy, on the surface, as he ate
his breakfast with his wife and walked the straight
and narrow, ready for a morning stroll;
though in the wall there was a tiny hole
through which he peered to see his brother's fate.

The East Berliner, not allowed to yell
how much he wanted bread was forced to fast
six days a week, and also had to run
around in circles in his prison cell.
But now the wall is crashing down at last;
the city of Berlin is really one.

SILENCE NO MORE

No more the stifled voice. No more green tea
instead of coffee, strong and dark. No more
denying that behind your closet door
wild orchids bloom. No more embroidery
of lies. No more endeavoring to be
the person you had planned to be before
you saw night's bonfire burning on your shore.
No more the silence of a surfless sea.

But if you're still ashamed to say out loud
those words you know you ought to say, then write
them down and let your pages speak instead
of you. Your closet's grateful shadows crowd
around you, thankful for your lantern's light
allowing them to resurrect the dead.

THE OUTING

This is the beginning of the end, here
and now I'm writing down the epilogue
to clarify the gray and cloudy; fog
disperses, leaving a bright blue sky where
the sun blazes down. Everything is clear
or will be clear quite soon. Pity the dog
under the bed, frightened someone will flog
him, pity the dog of Truth, hiding in fear.

Out, shadows, as I smash the closet door.
Out, mermen, out of the sea as I call
you, one by one, to stand where you've never stood
before. Out, Martians, two by two. No more
the closet of deception—burn it all,
shelf by blasted shelf, burn it, burn its wood.

INVESTIGATION

      closet window   closet door   closet men
who spend a lifetime looking for a key
to open up their closet   closet sea
     closet beach   closet seagulls circling when
we walk along the shore and count to ten
     ten seagulls   ten palm-trees   ten blankets we
have spread upon the sand beneath each tree
     closet ink   closet paper   closet pen

     closet midnight   closet moon   closet star
ten times ten shadows whisper, "*know thyself*"
ten times ten shadows help a closet sleuth
to solve the mystery of who we are
     closet fingerprints on a closet shelf
     closet magnifying glass   closet truth

WHAT WILL REMAIN?

A hundred years from now, what will remain
from costumes shadows wore, from flames that burned
behind a closet door, from seas which churned
incessantly throughout the night, from rain
that wouldn't stop, from a meadow and a plain
where purple orchids grew, from eyes which spurned
an outstretched hand, from mannequins who yearned
to touch the wind outside their window pane?

What will remain? Not very much: a book
of cindered words; a torn, discarded glove
a shadow sewed; a cage in which a bird
had lived and died, a rusty closet-hook;
a wind—and in that wind, the echo of
Apollo's dolphin's laughter, barely heard.

WE ARE

we are the shadows in his closet   we
are raveled threads that stitch together seams
of trouser cuffs with lies which truth redeems
we are the prison guards who set him free
we are his bottles of red wine   the key
that opens up the vault in which his dreams
are stored   we are the pebbles in his streams
we are night's mermen waiting in his sea

come to us   we whisper in the dark   come
to us and live   take off your coat   untie
your shoes   please try to feel at home   we'll give
you instruments to play   a gong   a drum
a pair of tambourines   just come and lie
with us   we beg him   bless him   curse him   live